God Smiled on Me...

Watch Me Rise

Charlotte Pinkney

God Smiled on Me...Watch Me Rise

Published in the United States of America

Sunshine Solutions Publishing
9912 Business Park Dr., Ste. 170
Sacramento, CA 95827

Library of Congress Control Number: 2019909201

ISBN-13: 9781078383820

Acknowledgements

I'd like to thank my children for all the love. They didn't believe in me at first. They said I was crazy for having big dreams. They see it happening now. I hope they see that I have faith down in my spirit. I've had dreams where God showed me what I am going to have. I share it with them all the time.

I'd like to thank my employers and colleagues for the support. Thanks to my great ministry for the prayers. Thank you for always lifting me up. Thanks to my neighbor. Thank you to the hater who told me to do it because they didn't really think I could. I know not everybody is going to be happy for me. For those that are, thank you. My big pastor is my biggest fan. Thank God for you.

I know God sent me to that church for a reason. I'm so grateful that you prayed for me and encouraged me not to give up. Thank you for your love and prayers pastor. My boss is another huge fan of my work. He promised to share my book with everyone he knows. That's love.

Thank you so much God! You blessed me in so many ways, even when I didn't know how I was going to make it. You would tell me not to worry. Thank you to so many others. I want to thank all of you for loving and supporting my book, and my other visions. God bless you all. I hope you enjoy reading about my life. I hope you will also see how awesome God is and that he will do it for you too. Just trust and believe He means what He says in his word.

Table of Contents

Growing Up

This is my story about growing up in a dark country city named Palatka, in Florida with my mom, brother and sister in a two-bedroom house. My mom would wake up early and cook for everyone. Afterward, she would sit my sister and I down and press our hair. Although she used to put a lot of grease on our foreheads and sometimes burn our ears, we looked so pretty after she finished so we didn't mind. We'd get ready for school. I would go next door to my friend Kimberly's. Kimberly and I used to play together. Afterwards, mom would see us off to school, before setting out for work where she cleaned houses.

She worked very hard to feed us. We didn't always have food to eat so we would go to the neighbor's house. I remember making sandwiches with just syrup and bread or eating a lot of peanut butter. It tasted so good. When my mom got paid, she would cook great things, like beans and rice with ham hocks and cornbread. We would eat till our stomachs were full, and we were always so happy.

We didn't have a lot of clothes or shoes. I remember having just two or three pairs of shoes. One of them had a big hole, but I was proud of my holey shoes and the clothes that I did have. I was so grateful for what we had.

Mom would take us downtown to see the parade at Christmas time. We loved seeing all the lights. The lights made me feel free. We would go back home to rest and share what we saw at the parade and then ask mom for things for Christmas.

My mom has two sisters. One lives in San Francisco and the other in New York. She also has two brothers. One lives in San Francisco and we don't know the whereabouts of the other one. My Uncle Eddy died. He used to show us a lot of love. He always took us shopping. I remember that he seemed to love younger women. He always made me laugh. My Auntie Carrie is my angel. You will see why as you read on.

My siblings and I used to share a room, but I slept with my mom. She was my best friend and a great mother. My mom worked so hard to give us what we needed the best way she knew how. Bless her heart. She was a strong-willed woman. I never knew my grandmother or grandfather, but I heard great things about them both. I recall being told they were also hard workers. I believe that's where my mom got that from. My uncle was like that too. He worked at the Mark Hopkins Hotel for almost 30 years. The hotel is one of the beautiful places to see in Florida. We had never seen the inside of a hotel as nice as that. The way my uncle used to show us around that place always felt so special. I give thanks for that particular blessing. Now, to the next chapter of my childhood.

I remember my mom talking on the phone, with her sister who lived in San Francisco, about how she needed to go to the doctor. She had been experiencing chest pains. She thought it could just be that she was working too hard. She didn't really think it was anything serious, which was probably why she was laughing so loud. Her sister probably said something hilarious. My dad was a great dad to me. I could trust him even though he was a heavy drinker who spent a lot of time playing cards with his friends. He made sure I stayed safe.

I am so grateful that my dad and mom allowed me to go to church. I was drawn to it from an early age. I would hear the singing and ask my mom if I could please go there. It was like something was pulling me there and the first time I attended church, it felt so comforting. The people were so nice and they served the best food after church. They let you have seconds too! I was always very happy to be there and completely enjoyed the preacher's message. You'd often find people yelling and jumping around and crying. The people were just happy to be there. As a child, I didn't understand what they were saying because they were speaking a language I didn't know. I went home to ask my mom what kind of talk that was. "Honey sit down. That's how people in church praise GOD. It's called speaking in tongues. That's how the Baptist Church is ok? Don't be afraid because it's alright", mom said. I let my mom know I wasn't afraid. I just wanted to know what was happening so that when I went back next week I wouldn't be in the dark. I was very happy for the opportunity to hear nice songs, eat some nice food and meet new friends after church. One sister came over to me and asked me if I would like to be a member of the church and I told her I would have to check with my mom first. They had a children's choir. She saw how much I enjoyed the service, she also asked me if I had ever been baptized. I said I had not and asked what it meant to be baptized. The sister said holy water is used as a renewal for healing and covering over your young life. I was amazed and told her I would need to ask my mom. I wanted to go into the holy water. I asked my mom for permission and she said, "Yes you can baby if you want to". I was so elated because I loved going to church. Going to church felt like a separate part of my life.

My brother and sister wanted to know why I kept going to church. I told them I liked going to church because I enjoyed it and that the people are nice to me. I invited them to come with me. Neither of them came. I told them I was getting baptized and explained why they needed to come with me into the water. I tried explaining how wonderful getting baptized was going to be. I even tried convincing them by telling them about the good food we would eat afterward. Truthfully those ladies over at the church cooked some good food, cakes, and pies too. I was very happy when I got baptized. Things were going well.

It was maybe a couple of years later when my dad was on his way to the bar to hang out with his friends when a barking dog would not leave him alone. He kept telling the dog to go away. Out of nowhere, the dog attacked him. The dog bit him on his leg, and it was very deep, it went down to his bone. My mother was so upset she kept on cursing and asking, "Whose dog is that?" Some woman said it was her dog. She kept saying sorry, but my mom told her that wasn't good enough. They were yelling at each other, and I was crying. My dad was in pain. My mom didn't take him to the hospital. We went home and poured whiskey on it to stop the pain. My dad just wanted to rest, so he did. My mom was still fussing. She wanted to fight the lady talking on the phone, but then she calmed down. Thank God! I was about 8 or 9 years old then.

A couple of years after that, my dad got sick. We took him to the hospital this time because he had a high fever. I recall thinking to myself that he had a horrible bite. The doctor gave him some medication because his leg was infected. He did get better. So, we were a happy family again. Thank God!

A Time of Loss

I had a stepbrother named Lionel. He was already a grown man when I was a little girl. He seemed larger than life. There were so many people around him, men and women who drove big cars with tinted windows and shiny rims. They wore big hats and flashy clothes. The women wore short dresses, high heels and big wigs with bright red lipstick. Smiling at me, one of the ladies said "You are so cute. You look like your big brother." I remember asking the lady, "Why do you wear those tall shoes and short dresses?" She said to me, "Baby I am doing what I have to do. You wouldn't understand. You are too young. Just stay in school and don't ever get into this life. It's not safe. Stay in school and listen to your mom."

My brother told the ladies to get inside the car. It was time to go to work. Then he came over to me and gave me a big hug. He told me he loved me a lot and that he was going out for a while with those ladies, but he would be back later. I said. "Okay brother, love you and be careful." I didn't know that would be the last time I saw my big brother alive.

A lady came running to our house screaming and knocking very hard on our door. She shouted, "Come now. Your brother is stuck inside his car and there is a lot of smoke inside.

The doors are jammed." At this point, we were not really thinking clearly. Nobody thought to break the windows. When we finally tried to break it, the windows wouldn't break. Wow! We didn't understand what the hell was happening. That was crazy. By the time the firemen came to open the car door, the gas fumes had already taken over. My brother died trapped inside the car from a gas leak. I believe the man he was fighting with earlier that day killed my brother over money. My dad told him to stay away from those men because they were jealous of him and he should not trust them. But young people don't often listen to their parents when it's best for them.

That really hurt me a lot, but God brought me through it. I'm grateful to God for the little time I was able to share with him. That experience showed me how he made some bad choices that resulted in the loss of his life. Things could have been different if he had listened to our dad.

The Father I Knew

This chapter is about my awesome dad. . My dad never seemed the same after my brother's death. I comforted him as much I knew how because I was just a little girl. The only thing I knew to do was to give him lots of hugs and tell him that I loved him every day. My dad was my friend. He would play ball with me and watch me while I skated down the street with my best friend from next door. Overall, my dad was a great man. He worked at the railroad track plant. I remember him fighting t with my mom because he had other kids with another woman and how she used to chase after him even though she knew he lived with us. The other woman was constantly after him and that caused problems between my mom and dad. One day my parents got into a big argument about my dad and the other woman. My mom told the other lady to stay away, but she didn't. I think my dad felt bad because he started to drink even more. The stress from his son dying and two women stressing him out was a lot to handle. I was the baby of the family, the last of all his children so he always made sure I had everything I needed while he was around. But he got tired of fighting with my mom, so he moved out to be with the other lady. I asked why he did that because my mom still loved him. They kept going back and forth, fighting with each other. I kept telling my dad that I loved him and asked him not to stop coming to see me because we were close. He still came to see me. I was so happy because I was a daddy's girl.

One day, my friend and I were playing school with our baby dolls and drinking tea. We pretended to grade our student's homework because we were both teachers. A woman came by and told me my dad had just been bitten by a dog. She said he needed help right away, so I yelled for my mom to come help my dad. I was crying when we reached my dad because I could see that he was in so much pain. The bite was really deep into his leg. My mom didn't want to take my dad to the hospital. Some firemen came and helped clean his leg. Mom said he couldn't go to the doctor. I don't know why. We went home although he was still in a lot of pain. My dad was bitten so badly. The bite went all the way to the bone. I think his leg probably got infected because he didn't go to the doctor. My mom just kept cleaning it with whiskey. I kept praying that God would heal my dad's leg. He rested a while. Later he started having pain again, but he still didn't go to the doctor. A month later he went back to work and we were all happy again and doing things together as a family. The yelling subsided and our neighbors were happy that they no longer had to contend with the loud noise coming from our home.

My friend and I went back outside with our toys. We were having a great time. I noticed that my dad sometimes seemed worried. I guess he was thinking about my brother being gone. My mom and I were walking to the grocery store one day when we saw my dad. He came over to us, gave me a hug and a kiss then told me he loved me. My mom asked him for money to get extra food to cook. We said we would see each other later at the house for dinner. My dad loved fried chicken. I asked my mom if I could get some ice cream. She said I could. We kept shopping while talking about how good dinner was going to taste. We were so happy walking back home. The next thing I knew, someone was running towards us, yelling and crying for us to wait. They said something bad had happened to my dad. They said my dad was found dead inside a ditch. I didn't say anything. I was so quiet that the person asked me if I was okay. I told them that couldn't be because we just saw my dad. I explained how we were talking with him before we went to the store. I couldn't believe it. My mom wasn't saying anything. She was in shock. She couldn't believe it either. I kept asking what happened. I wanted to know if anybody saw anything. I begged them to tell me.

It was all too much. I was out of my mind. I asked God why my brother had to go and now my dad. I was just a little girl. I didn't understand what was going on. When we talked to the police we asked if someone could die from falling into a dry ditch. It all seemed impossible because we were just talking with him. He was fine. He hugged and kissed both of us. I was distraught and I asked God why my daddy had to go.

I began to talk to God. I told him I didn't know what he was doing, but I know he always has a plan. I prayed and asked him not to take any more loved ones away from me because I was just a little girl. I couldn't understand why someone would want to hurt my dad. I loved my dad so much. He was the only dad in our home. My sister and brother didn't know my dad like I did. I asked God to please watch over my family. Praying gave me strength.

I let God know I trusted him. I thanked him for his grace and mercy. Now we are going through another death. This is truly devastating. All we can do is pray our way through. Lord, I know you are watching over me because I am ok. Although I miss my dad, I am going back to church to ask the pastor to pray for my family. I am so thankful that I am connected to a church family. This was a huge part of my life growing up.

My Mother's Love

This part of the story is more touching because it's about my beautiful mom. I thank God for her. She was a great mom. She truly loved all her children. She did her best. We had a routine where, every morning we'd wake up, wash our faces, brush our teeth, comb our hair and the girls will get a warm press. There was always a lot of grease on my forehead and I remember getting my ears burned because my mom would get too close with the hot-comb. It was very hot and telling her that was like saying the sun is shining outside. Then would get dressed and eat breakfast. We would have cold cereal if we had it, but sometimes we had grits and fried pork chops or catfish. We didn't always have food. Sometimes we would make syrup sandwiches. The sandwiches were so good, and we had lots of Kool-Aid. We loved that and still do. We ate whatever we had. We were happy to. We never rejected food offered to us. We were thankful to have something to eat at all and didn't complain.

I only had two pairs of shoes, and one pair had a hole in it but I was thankful. My mom didn't have a lot of money because she used to clean houses. She made most of the dresses worn by my sister and I . My mom could make nice dresses without any pattern. Being clean was important to her. She would wash our clothes and give us baths. It was tough on us with my dad being dead. It was really hard for my mom, but she was a very strong woman. She never stopped working and trying to be the best mom she knew how.

Over time it became too much for her. Without anybody to help her, she started drinking to deal with the pain of my dad not being there. I remember her yelling at my dad a lot, but they also had some good times playing cards together. One of our favorite family games was spades. That was so much fun. Sometimes I would cry because my dad was my friend and he was gone, but my mom would give me a hug and I would feel better.

My mom would get angry at times about having to fight with the social security office to get money to help care for my siblings and I . It was hard. Her stress was getting out of control. She needed to rest. So, she did.

My mom had some family in San Francisco and New York. She had two sisters and two brothers. We had an older sister, who also had a daughter. She didn't visit often because she and my mom always fought. My mom didn't like her husband either, but she loved her granddaughter very much. My mom's sister would go to Florida and bring nice things for her and to help her out with bills, which I think was great. My mom was always sad when her sister left. I had an aunt who lived in San Francisco, and was always asking my mom if she could take me home with her. My mom would say, "No that's my baby." At the time I didn't understand why she asked that of her. We had fun listening to the war stories from when they were little. I was always sad when it was time for my auntie to leave. She was always so nice to me and my friend next door.

One day my mom said she didn't feel good, so later that night we told her to lay down and rest and then we went into the living room to watch tv. We laughed like kids do when having a good time. After a while, we had to turn the tv off because we had school in the morning. That night I prayed to God to heal my mom's body because my stepbrother was gone and my daddy too. I pleaded with him not to take my mom. I didn't know who would take care of me if she was gone. "Lord, please don't take my mom away. I need her. You gave her to me to protect my sister and brother," I prayed. After that, she got better. I thanked God for healing her body.

I have such fond memories of growing up. I remember one day when my friends and I were riding our bikes, having so much fun. We got thirsty and decided to go inside to get a drink of water. Afterward, we went across the street to the store to buy big lemon cookies that cost only ten cents. Wow, this was a big deal to me as a kid. My friend and I went back home to eat our cookies. . Mom made dinner and it smelled good. She was cooking smothered pork chops, rice, cornbread, and collard greens. Dinner was going to be good. It was time to come inside, wash our hands and get ready for dinner. We usually came together to pray before eating as a family. It was so great sharing stories about what happened during the day at school and how my mom's day was. We were not allowed to watch too much tv. We talked more and read books. After dinner, we had to get ready for the next day. That meant taking a bath, brushing our teeth, and praying to wake up. The next day I went through my morning routine of getting ready for school, hugging my mom and telling her how much I love her, then off to school with my friend. Sometimes we would get a ride from her mom. My mom would go to work to clean houses. I would think of her on the way, hoping she has a great day.

My sister and brother are older than me. I am the baby of the family. I would come home from school so happy because I had a good day. My mom was often very tired after a hard day at work. She was resting one day, and it looked to me like she was in pain. I asked if she was okay and if she needed anything. She said she didn't need anything and that I should just do my homework. Once my brother and sister got home, we were supposed to work together to fix dinner. I told her I would, but I was worried about her. My sister warmed the leftovers so we could eat. We tried our best to help out in our different ways. Mom was tired and we let her rest because she needed it.

We usually made mom's plate first and then said grace before we ate. Having meals together is one of my favorite memories from my childhood. We would tell stories about our day, then help clean up afterward. Washing dishes and sweeping the kitchen floor was just a normal part of our day. It's what we had to do at our house. Sometimes we ate dessert. I loved sweets. I kept asking her if she felt ok since she got some rest. She kept saying she was fine and not to worry about her. My mom would tell me how much she loved me and my siblings. She said we were the reason she had to live. She loved seeing smiles on our faces every day and told us that was the greatest gift she could ever receive.

One night after finishing our chores she told us she was going to take a bath and then lay down. We talked and laughed together while watching tv. I think we were too loud because mom asked us to quiet down. She said she was having chest pains. This was getting scary. I told my mom we needed to go to the hospital to get checked out. We needed to know what was happening. Lord knows I didn't understand what was going on. I was just a little girl. All the deaths in my family affected me a lot, especially because they occurred when I was quite young. I knew deep down that everything would be alright. God is always in control.

We were sitting at the hospital waiting for the doctor to come to tell us what was going on with our mom. He told us they were still running some tests and asked us to wait a little longer. He said she was going to be fine and not to worry. Then he asked where my dad was, and I told him he died a couple of years before. The doctor said he was sorry for my loss and now understood why I was so worried about my mom. I thanked him and told him I was going to keep praying for God to watch over her because she was a gift he gave to us. She was there to watch over us and protect us I explained. After about 30 minutes, the doctor came back and said we could take mom home. They couldn't find anything wrong. He said it may have just been gas moving around or maybe it was my prayer. It seemed like God listened to my prayers he said.

Mom came out smiling and hugging us, and telling us how much she loved us. She said she felt great and she didn't feel any more pain in her chest. She was different. We couldn't understand it. I told her I was praying for her to feel better and she did. I thanked God for not taking her away from us because we needed her and wanted her around. She was a great mom. When we came home from school mom was so happy, she kept on telling us how much she loved us and that we should be good. We asked her why she was talking like that. We asked if she was going somewhere and she said she wouldn't go anywhere without us. She was dancing around and she looked happier than we thought was normal. We wondered if the doctor had given her some kind of medication that he didn't tell us about. She didn't say he gave her anything. We just kept watching her and asking her what was going on. We were thankful to God for making her better and taking away her pain. I really didn't understand, but God knew what was going on and that was enough for me. We just kept praying and telling her we loved her. I slept with her so I could be close to her.

I remember saying good morning to her when I woke up in the morning and how she didn't say anything back. So, I touched her and told her to wake up, but she didn't. She had been so happy the night before. I ran to my brother and sister's room and told them mom wasn't waking up. I told them to call for help. I was crying and yelling at that point. I asked the Lord why he would take my mom away too. I wanted to know why he would take everyone from me. I was just a little girl. I didn't understand what else I could have done. I went back into the room, but she was as cold as an ice cube. My mom had died during the night. I figured that's why she kept saying she loved us so much.

My mom was my best friend. We did a lot of things together. I ran next door to tell the neighbor that my mom had passed on. She cried. Her family came from all over to comfort us. We called our older sister who was married and living with her husband at the time. She called my mom's two sisters, the one in San Francisco who was my angel from God and my mom's other sister who lived in New York. My mom had two brothers who lived in San Francisco too. We had only met one of them. It was all so upsetting. I was crying , trying to figure out where we were going to go. I was hurt and angry.

After some time, I went back to my normal routine, going to the mall with my friends and going to the movies. I was just trying to be a happy teen, but that didn't stop me from thinking about all the storms I had been through. I had decided to make my life count. I wanted to experience joy because I knew I couldn't be angry forever. I needed to fight for my independence to be a great young lady because I knew God loved me. I know my mom and dad are looking down on me and saying, "Good job daughter. We are proud of you. Keep going, learn all you can and stay in church always."

I thank God for the awesome time we shared and for the opportunity to know you. Mom, I will love you forever. It just hurts so bad, but I am growing and trusting in everything.

A Reflection of Who I Am

I have the power to do what needs to be done and be who I am meant to be as long as I stay close to God. Have you ever asked yourself what you are doing or why you are thinking in a certain way? Whenever I find myself in that situation, I tell myself to get my mind right because I know this is not right. I ask the Lord to help me get back on track. I know when I'm close to my blessing. I say a prayer of thanks to God for getting me back on track.

I don't like to fail, but I pray to stay the course. I want so many things in my life. I have big visions and I know it's totally God because a lot of amazing blessings are coming my way. Only God can put these kind of visions in me. I am ready to receive and waiting for the breakthrough that God promised me

When young mothers come to me with their problems, I pray for them and with them. I enjoy supporting them. They come when they need housing or food. I don't mind reaching out to them with love. Just seeing the smile on their faces brings joy to my heart because I want to help them and their children in any way I can. That is part of my vision. I want to provide a place where they can feel safe with their children and have food to eat every day. I want them to be able to take a shower and feel like they belong to a family. I am praying that someday; I can open a home just for this. I want to be a resource for them and encourage their children to stay in school. Being able to give back is a blessing. God is always putting people that need help in my life. My purpose is to serve single moms.

I didn't realize this until I got to this point in my life. I didn't realize it was a ministry because it's what I do naturally, and I enjoy it so much. I am hoping that by sharing my story, I'll be able to help another woman. I have a vision. The only thing that holds us back is our unwillingness to step out of the box. You must have faith. I know my blessings are on the way. I am just practicing right now so when I get my blessing, I'll be ready to handle it. I know God wants to bring out greatness in me. I believe that's why things are so crazy now, but I intend to remain prayerful while I get ready. I cry sometimes because I am happy and because I've been through so much and I'm still standing. It's a blessing to be able to share all my life with the world. I am grateful for God's love in my life.

Childhood Memories

I often think about some of the things that happened when I was a little girl. So many memories of growing up come to mind. I remember how I fell down while I was skating and bruised my knees. I remember bike riding with my friend Kimberly who lived next door. I loved her so much. We played together. We enjoyed watching people across the street in the housing project. They were always doing something entertaining. We liked watching the nice cars drive by and walking down the long dirt road listening to the train bells ringing. Sadness would often set in because I wanted my mom back. I kept thinking it was a bad dream. I remember my sisters and brothers arguing about who's going to take care of us.

I heard my auntie from New York saying she wasn't going to take all three of us bad ass kids. That's when my angel sent from God said her sister wouldn't want her children split up. She said we needed to stay together. She said she would take us back to San Francisco with her. She felt it was the right thing to do. I was so happy because I didn't want to go with my other auntie who lived in New York. She was mean. I was still feeling lost and numb because it just didn't feel real. We didn't have anything to worry about. We went with my auntie and uncle who lived in San Francisco. I thank God for our angel. At that point, people were doing what people do in time of loss and grief, they argued about who would get the jewelry and other objects that I didn't care anything about. I just wanted my mom back. I didn't know what to do or to think anymore. My great auntie comforted me because I was the baby girl, just like my mom she was the baby sister.

When we left Florida, it was our first time on an airplane. We had only seen a plane flying in the sky or on the tv. My auntie had a big beautiful house. We were so happy. We never had our own room before. I was so grateful to God. I had my own bed, my own dresser, and my own tv. Wow! I felt like a princess. My auntie enrolled us in school and took us shopping. . She was great. She even rewarded me when I got good grades. I didn't really know my cousins. They used to look at us like we were aliens or something. I used to get angry when they asked questions about our mom's death, but then I would calm down after a while. I told them the story. They sometimes tried to pull some slick stunts, but I let them know I didn't play like that. I may have been young, but I saw right through them. I still had a lot of anger because I didn't understand why I had to lose all my family members within such a short time. I started drinking and fighting with people because I was hurt. I couldn't focus on my schoolwork at the beginning, but I stopped doing those things after a while because I didn't like the way it made me act out. I gradually started making friends. They thought they could play games with me because I was from Florida, but I showed them.

When I got older, I started dating. I asked my auntie to direct me to the church because I loved to hear the word of God and the singing brought me so much joy. I found a church I liked and met a nice family. I kept going back and going to bible study, and that really kept me strong. As time passed, I learned that not everybody around me had my best interest at heart. People are often mean for no reason, like making fun of my hair or clothes or just being mean. I didn't let that stop me from being focused on what I needed to do for my life because I knew I had to make a change for the better. That meant no matter what I had to stay close to the church.

After a while I started thinking I didn't need to go to church. I was beginning to skip Sunday service with the excuse that I would go the next week. I started hanging out with the wrong crowd and getting myself into things that weren't good for me. I used to be a good judge of character, but somehow, I got off track. Then one day I met this person and I started hanging out with her and spending time with her. We used to do a lot of things together, go everywhere together, we were practically like sisters. Then one day she made me face my anger and told me I had to forgive my mom for leaving me so soon. I listened to her and forgave my mom, which helped me appreciate all the memories we shared and I learned to cherish them more.

God's Love

I read from my bible and I pray daily for strength to make it through so I can be a blessing to others and serve and help people within every area of life. Most importantly, I believe God is love.

I have to make sure the people around me love God. We must work together in love so that his greatness will be exposed to the world. God is responsible for bringing out this part of me. He saw the best in me. I'm waiting on my hookup and I know it is coming. This is my time. Even when things look as if nothing is changing, God is working it out for my good. I tell my children to pray about everything and trust only God because a lot of people will let you down and leave you when you need help the most. God won't. It doesn't matter what it is, God will never leave you no matter how bad things get. You could lose your job, your place or even have your spouse walk out on you. Many people won't be there to help or listen, but God will see you through and love you without judgment.

I have to keep working towards my purpose. I don't know how many steps it's going to take to get there, but I'm going to keep stepping forward with love and a smile knowing that God will meet me there with a blessing. I just have to trust in him and have faith. Some people say I'm crazy, but it's ok because I am not in this by myself. God is with me. I think we are all crazy in some way. Nevertheless, I am moving forward. I have come too far to stop now. I have faith that everything is going to be alright because I am blessed, and I can bless others. We need to love each other and encourage one another at all times. We must also place ourselves in the right position to receive our blessings. To do that, I have to maintain my prayer life. Wanting to be a blessing to others is a great vision. I am learning something great about myself at every turn. I didn't know I had it in me. I'm so thankful for my gifts and for the ability to share them with others. I need to watch my steps and the way I talk and how I live my life. I am experiencing a shift in my life and I don't want to repeat any of the negative things I've been through because it was very painful the first time. Whew! Thank you, God, for all of my blessings. Like I said before, I just have to keep praying my way through. I have learned not to make choices without praying first because when I do, it doesn't turn out right. This journey has been a challenge for me, but I remember that God is on my side. I am going to make it and I know he sees the hard work I am putting out.

I'm hoping this story helps and blesses women all over the world. If God blessed me through it, he will do it for you too. Just trust and believe you are worth it. Sometimes when we get hurt by people, we might not understand it at the time, but eventually you will. Today I learned to trust more. I wanted to be a part of something , and I spoke it out loud. Because I have faith and trust that God listens to my prayers, I was able to step out and see my blessings manifested. I never knew I could be this strong.

It's hard to go on sometimes. I wish my mom was here for me even if it's just to say something as simple as, "I'm home. What are we having for dinner?" I'd love to be able to tell her in person that I appreciate all the things she taught me - to brush my teeth, to comb my hair, to take a bath every day because being stinky is not the business, to keep a clean house at all times, wash my clothes regularly, wash my hands before cooking and to just be clean in everything I do. I learned to treat people the way I want to be treated because she taught me that. I will never forget these lessons. My commitment to the church has carried me through so much. I will always keep God first. He is the reason I am a living miracle. I know I could not have made it without him.

My mom couldn't afford much. Having nice things isn't out of my reach. I know through God I can have the nice things I desire. God says that if you can envision it, you can have it. I have learned to forgive my mom and dad for not being there. I know now that having them for such a short time doesn't make me a lesser person. Today I am great. Prayer has helped my growth. I understand it's not about me. It's about God. I always keep him first. I believe great blessings will come into my life because he looks at what is in my heart. I want good things for people. I love to help people. Doing this fills me with happiness .

Seeing the smile on the face of a young mom who came to me for help made me feel so good. She had been talking to her three-year-old son about having some soup, but didn't know how to make it nor did she have the ingredients to put it together. So, I told her how to make it and then went to the store to get her some food. When I brought her the food, she was so happy. She couldn't believe I would do that. She was so thankful. I told her it was my pleasure and God Bless. I let her know that I know what it's like to not have what you need. People were kind enough to help me, so I help others when I can too. I like giving to encourage the young moms. I experienced similar things. It wasn't easy, but I made it through God's s grace.

Lessons Growing Up

I can remember the first time I moved out. There were good times and hard times. I was so happy to be doing it on my own. I liked being able to fix my place up the way I wanted. It was small and quiet. I had nice neighbors. I was trying to prove something to myself. I got myself a car and a washer and dryer to keep my clothes clean. Wow, the memories! My auntie wanted me to come back home, but I wasn't having it. I wanted to see the world for myself. I would buy groceries, cook a nice dinner and eat. Sometimes I had company, but not much because I didn't like having too many people around. I was low key. I started going to city college part time while working and paying my own bills. I was very independent. I wanted a man who was the same way, but it didn't work out like that. I was enjoying my life. At first, I was focused on my education. Then, I met this handsome man. This has always been my weakness.

I wanted to be a nurse because I had worked at Mary's Hospital as a candy striper. I assisted the nurses with bathing patients, walking and feeding them, but I eventually changed my goals. I started taking child development classes and became a preschool teacher. I really enjoy serving the young moms. They tell me about their relationship problems, family and baby daddy drama and I prayed with and for them. I share my experiences with them so they can see what I've been through. I want them to know I survived it to encourage them so they can look for ways to help themselves. I want them to know they can make it.

I remember how my girlfriend and I were riding around the city, smoking and thinking we were the finest women around. My friend said she needed to pick something up and I agreed to go with her. When we got to the house where the something was, I saw this dude looking out the window at me and waving. I was thinking to myself that I hope he doesn't think I want him. Of course, he comes outside and says hi, then says he heard I was from the south. I just sat there looking at him for a minute before finally replying that I was. He kept trying to talk to me, but I wasn't really feeling him. I told him I didn't talk to men I didn't really know. The whole situation just didn't sit right with me. I kept wondering where my friend was. Finally, she came out of the house. Of course, the same man who was trying to talk to me came out with her. I could tell he wasn't a good man, so I told my friend I was ready to go.

I noticed more men coming up to this house. I noticed that one of them was fine and that made me smile because I do love a handsome and tall man. My dad was a tall, handsome man. We made eye contact and then he spoke to me. I told him my name. He said I was cute and that he liked the way I talked. He asked where I was from and I told him. We exchanged numbers, but I could see something wasn't right. When I got home, my friend called me and told me that the same man that was trying to talk to me had shot someone at that house.

This is what I mean about faith. I know the holy spirit saved me from that situation. I thanked God for his grace. I had stopped going to church for a while, but that experience made me feel like I needed to start going back. I'm not saying that this happened because I left the church. Things do happen for no apparent reason. I do know that God gives me insight when danger is close. However, I've noticed that when I'm close to the church and prayerful, bad things don't occur as much around me or to me. So, I started going back to church.

Everyone was so happy to see me back. I joined the church choir. I enjoyed being a part of the church family. I did learn that not everyone at church is good and sometimes they did things I knew wasn't right. This didn't stop me from going to church. I needed the word to feed me. I liked going to sing at other churches and the fellowship was always great.

When I was about to graduate, I thought I knew enough about how to survive on my own. I had a little job and had saved some money and I had the trust account my auntie set up for me. It was a lot and I wasn't mature enough to do the right thing with money to make it work for me in the long term.

My auntie kept trying to tell me how to handle money, but I didn't listen to her. When you're young you think you know everything, but I learned the hard way that I didn't. I wish I hadn't put myself through that. If only I had listened to her. I would not have suffered so bad, but through constant prayers and having God rooted in my life I knew I would make it. So, I started looking for my own place to prove to myself that I can make it on my own. I sometimes thought about mom, wondering if she was looking down on me and I hoped that I had become the young lady my dad hoped I would be.

I've made a lot of mistakes, but I am learning from each one of those mistakes in order to make better choices next time. I thank my mom for teaching me to never give up. I miss and need her so much. I remember her being a hard worker and a good friend to me. She was my best friend. My mom was someone I could talk to and tell what I feel, and I'll always be grateful to her for being the kind of mother that listened. I know she will always look over me because I'm her baby.

I learned that the only difference between me and anyone else is the way I look at life. Neither of us will look at things the same way. I don't want what my sister or brother has. I just want what God has for me. My blessings have survived everything I have been through. I don't believe my children could have survived what I went through. I know that everything God has saved me from is for his purpose and for me to be a blessing to someone else. It has taught me to open my mind. An open mind gives you a better outlook on life. There are people who can't stop complaining even when you offer them help. It is quite tiresome and sucks all the air out of my balloon. I can only take so much. Giving this over to God because I know he will see me through even as I continue to run this race. I am staying focused on his word now.

I remember wanting to buy some new furniture and lamps and going down to Mission Street to get them. I tried hard to keep nice things. I started inviting people over because I was happy about my new success. However, I noticed when they left that some things were missing. I was in shock. I couldn't believe it. This experience is why I don't like having many people around. I told the Lord I had decided that I would keep some people at a distance.

You would think that I would have learned my lesson, but no, I am back to hanging out with my friend with whom I did everything . I know I said I wouldn't ride with her anymore because the last time I did, a crazy man tried to talk to me and someone got shot. However, I found myself tagging along on her way to pick up her cousin. We were riding and singing out loud, having a good time, when she turns into a hotel property and I'm thinking to myself, "why are we here?" I see the same crazy man coming out. He was smiling and greets me, "Hey pretty lady." I say, "hi and reply that I'm fine." He says, "Oh I know how you look. Why don't you come on up?" I know deep down I shouldn't because this doesn't feel right, but he was being so nice. They were drinking and smoking while we were out. I was still trying to figure out why he was hanging around. He kept mentioning that I was from the south and wanting to know more about me. I told him about my parent's passing and he offered his condolences.

My friend warned me not to go anywhere with him. I thought it would be ok because he was acting better than he did the first time we met. I brushed it off and said it wasn't a big deal. We were just going out to eat. He came to pick me up and we went out to dinner. He kept looking at me and telling me how pretty I was. He asked me if I wanted to make fast money. I told him no because I had a job and was in college. He said that was okay, but I could make more than I did at my job. I told him no again, that I don't do those kind of things, and to take me home. He got close to my face and told me he wasn't taking me home and that I was going to spend the night with him so he could break me in. I got upset and said, "What the hell are you talking about?" He told me I was going to work for him. I told him I wasn't that way. While we were walking to the car, he was yelling at me, telling me I was going to do what he told me to. I told him I was not. I got in the car with him and realized I didn't know where we were.

He could tell I was nervous and about to bolt. He tried to comfort me by saying he was just playing with me. He would take me home after he made a quick stop, but at this point I was really scared. I didn't know who this man was or where he was taking me. It was our first date. The next thing I know we are at some house and he's introducing me to some man. I'm silently praying. They go back and forth about me being the woman from the south he

had talked about before. He told him my name.
The man smiled at me.

   I asked to use the restroom so I could use
my cell phone to make a call for help. I wanted
to tell my family what the car looked like and to
call the police. He knocked on the door and
asked me if I was ok. I told him I was and hung
up the phone. When I came out, he took me to a
room. I had already decided I wasn't going to
fight him because I didn't want to make it worse.
I didn't know if he had a gun or not. He talked
for a long time, crazy stuff because he was high.
After a while he was ready for sex. I kept saying I
was on my period. He didn't care. I told him he
didn't have to bring me way over here for sex. He
kept talking crazy. He promised to take me
home after. I played along. I told him I wanted
him too. I let him know my family was looking
for me. He told me I was talking too much. He
tried having sex with me, but he couldn't do
anything. He was too high. He got mad and
wanted me to help him. So, I did because he was
getting more upset. I didn't want him to hurt
me. while this was happening, I was secretly
praying for God to get me through this.
Thankfully, the whole thing only lasted a few
seconds. I was still playing the part to ensure my
safety. We laid down to sleep. He woke up in the
middle of the night and took me home. God
saved me. He heard my prayers. He will never let

me down. Prayer is so powerful. You must believe and trust Him. I believe He allows some things to happen so you will trust Him.

Surviving this trauma made me realize that I need to change my friends and my environment. That really opened my eyes. I learned to be careful about who I let into my life. Just because it looks good doesn't mean it will be. Wanting good things is fine, but you can't be blind to what you see. You can have better if you believe it will come to pass in good time.

Moving Forward

God had to move some people out of my life so I could move forward. I do believe they were there for a reason. Don't get stuck looking back. Just move forward. I have to work hard to stay focused and keep good people in my life. God gives me everything I need to get through everything. I just pray , and blessings abound. Only the strong survive. God made it so I could escape so I know I can handle whatever comes my way. Thank God for hope and faith. If I didn't believe in his strength, trust me that man would have killed me. That's why I want to bless many others with this message. God is faithful if you trust him with everything.

I stopped trusting people at that point in my life because trusting certain people could put me in a dangerous space. Thank God my mom always said to pray. She said if I did, God would bless me. Now, thinking back, sometimes I didn't know if I was going to eat or how I was going to pay my bills. Because I didn't listen to what my angel told me about putting up money, even if it's only a few dollars, it will eventually add up. Not listening to that advice made it so hard, but I knew I had another chance to do better. I did for a while. I've always seen myself having nice things. I truly believed I would because God said I can.

I am still living for my purpose. God knew that all these things would happen in my life and I hope that I have passed the tests he put in my path. My miracle is coming soon because I am faithful and a giver to others. I also serve at my church. I will keep serving and being a cheerful giver. I know that God didn't bring me through all these experiences not to bless me in a great way so that I may be a blessing to others. It's not about me. It's about him always. Thank you, God, for saving me again.

I just need to get my mind straight for my new beginning. I am staying prayerful and keeping my eyes wide open to see far out of the box. The time is coming and my due season to have what's part of my destiny is almost here. I know when God takes me higher people will go away because they won't understand it. I just have to stay faithful.

When I was a teen, I got a phone call from someone who found me in San Francisco. I don't know how they found me or the phone number to pass the message across that my stepsister and her children had been killed in Miami. She was in a car accident on the freeway. We had a good relationship. I cried and just sat on the couch and looked up. It felt like all my people were dying. I just didn't understand. I loved my stepsister and my nieces. I remember how she used to come to Palakta to see me. She would take me to the store and buy me some candy and tell me how much she loved me. She was nice to my mom also. That meant a lot to me as a little girl. It was very special to me that she made time for me. I loved her.

My auntie was such a wonderful angel. She asked me if I wanted to go to the funeral and I said I didn't want to. I told her I would be ok. I cried a lot. I asked God to hold me through and comfort me. He knew I had what it takes to overcome the hurt again. She told me to press my way through and keep praying to God. It's so awful for a young person to have so much death in their life. It was tough going to school and living through that. People wondered what had happened to me because I was gone for a bit. I told them about the bad news about my stepsister and her kids. Some of them commented about the number of deaths in my family. Others wanted to know what they could do. I told them to just pray for me and my family. After a while, it got to be too much, and I had to ask them to change the subject. Many offered me their condolences and I accepted them. I thanked them for their concern. Grieving is a difficult process. There were times when I was fine and times when I got so angry. I prayed and talked to God to ask for forgiveness.

All the networking I did last year is beginning to bear fruit. Everyone I reached out to lived far away. I didn't have the money to get to each city. Dreams really can come true. I didn't know how or when, but God came through for me. When I tell you that God will deliver, believe me. I never thought someone like me would be able to meet people I watch on tv. It was scary being able to look this person in the eye. All I can say is, "thank you." The other person God blessed me to meet is such a good person. I said I want to see her, and God put her in my path. She came off the stage right where I was sitting. I looked into her eyes and I saw God. I spoke about it and He brought her to me, and I even met her son. God has been so awesome in my life. That is, I am not ashamed to say it in this book He has done great things for me, my children and my family.

I thank God for giving me the privilege to be part of a great church and the best pastor in the world. I'm grateful to be connected to such great leadership. When you are working hard to make your vision come to be, God will use anybody to bless you. It doesn't have to be someone you know, or someone with an education or money because we all have different gifts to share with each other. Don't count someone out because of the way they look because that can be the very person God sent to help you with your vision. No matter what or who comes into your life, remember to show love because it's the right thing to do . I don't always understand what's going on around me, but I stay anchored in my prayer life because that's what keeps me moving forward. All the people who have passed through my life taught me a lesson on how to be stronger and not to repeat the behavior. If I hadn't experienced the things I did along my journey, I wouldn't be the woman I am today. I thank, God, for all my teachers.

I look back at my life and I can't help but thank God for the master plan he created for my life. The enemy tries to block my blessings, but God won't let it happen. He will always hide me away from harm. I am starting my journey by stepping out in faith. It's hard, but I will win because God already said I shall have it. I don't have to run away anymore. I am in a safe place that is filled with love. You can get through anything with love. I will survive. My mom taught us to fight back, work hard for what we want in life, and always pray for everything. I am learning to let God deal with my children. When I see them making wrong choices, I want to rescue them right away. However, I know that I must allow them to grow up. I don't want to see them hurt by people, but that's how moms are. I pray this book helps them. If you want to reach a goal, just pray about it and God will guide you through. Having kids is tough. You want to save them from everything. One day they need you to feed them and in what seems like the next day they're telling you how grown they are. They are my blessing. Nothing compares to the pain they have put me through now that they are older.

I'm completely focused on my journey to be a better woman and to help others. I love to help others with a willing heart. I regret trusting the wrong people in my life. I didn't always make good choices. I should have waited to hear God's voice, but being in such a hurry to change my situation caused me to forget that God sees all and is in control of everything. So, I suffered for not being patient. Now I know that God doesn't need my help with anything that's going on in my life or my children's lives. I am praying my way through each battle. I hope my children can see how I survived and know that when things are difficult , they can always count on God. They have seen how God has restored my life from the lowest level. I kept praying and He brought me back. I got a second chance to do better and do the work I love. When you think about everything God has let you survive, it is enough testimony for you to bless someone else. Whatever you are going through, just know I have seen Him do miracles. He will do it for you too, but you must believe. He won't fail you ever, no matter how we see in the natural. It is what we imagine in our spirit that is true for all. God gives me what I need and want in His time, not my time. I just have to be still and stay in His word in order to be strong. This is our weapon against anything that comes our way.

What I Know Now

When you love your children so much and give them more than they should have to replace the hurt someone else caused you, we must realize that this is not what God asked us to do. I didn't understand at the time, but I do now. This is why I can share my story with you. I am blessed to have lived through all the craziness and I'm still standing.

I still have more soul-searching to do deep down in my spirit. When you want to know if you are doing the right thing, God will show you. Don't be afraid. I used to be, but being closer to God makes you stronger. Every day I keep him first in my life, I pray every day and all day. That's what gets me through.

People can be cruel. Sometimes I come across people who talk bad about me, but I don't pay them any attention. I just smile and keep it moving. They look at me like I'm crazy because I smile even though they don't deserve my kindness. I just ask God to bless them. The hardest part is loving the people who lie right in your face.

I was so mad at myself for letting my husband come back and repeat the same behavior. Yes, I let him come back home again. I know you're wondering why I would do that. At the time, I didn't understand it myself. After all that happened, I kept forgiving him. I figured it was out of fear. When a man hits you so much, you eventually become fearful. Even when you get a restraining order, they keep coming back to "talk". If you are cheating and fighting all the time, you are obviously telling me you want to be free.

The final straw for me happened when I was pregnant with our daughter. I wanted to go to a singing program with him and he didn't want me to come. We started fighting about me going to church. Now you know it's crazy to want to stop anyone from going to church, but when you are a cheat and an abuser you don't care. I was eight or nine months pregnant. He pushed me and I hit him back. He grabbed me as I went down the door and pushed me again. I heard his phone ringing. He was so mad he forgot to turn his phone down and I could hear the girl on the phone saying she couldn't wait to see him. I started crying and praying right in my kitchen. I told the Lord I would not take this cheat and abuser back into my life if He saved me. Even after hearing her voice on the phone, he still tried to say that it was his homeboy on the phone. His brothers drove up and were honking for him to come out, but we were fighting. One of his brothers came to the door and told him to come on. He saw me crying and asked me what happened. I told him that his cheating brother didn't want me to go to the church program because he had another waiting for him. He couldn't believe he was doing this to me. He didn't care. He still talked crazy. He said I wasn't going anywhere. My stomach started hurting because I was upset and yelling at him. When his brother turned around, he punched me in my stomach. I thought my baby was dead because I stared bleeding. I was so mad I went to the kitchen drawer to look for a knife to kill him. His brother helped me to sit down and tried to calm me down While my husband continued to yell and swear at me. I told him I knew the reason he didn't want me to go was because he was still cheating. He was crazy as hell. I called my best friend to come with me to the hospital. I kept praying to God to give me the courage to never look back. I could have lost my beautiful daughter, but God didn't let it happen. She is so beautiful. I am so thankful to God I didn't die either.

It was tough. Bills were piling up. God has been so awesome in my life. I remember not having money to get anything for my daughter during Christmas. We were standing in line at the store when I saw my church member. She asked how I was doing and if I knew anyone who needed a food basket for the holidays. I said my neighbor did. God touched her to ask about me and my family. God did it. I started sharing with her about my money problems and she said the church will help me and that I should speak with the deacon. I went to church service and God blessed my family in a time of hardship . He has been so awesome in my life. This is why I love to serve and listen to whatever service I can so I can be a blessing to others.

If I don't know I will find out or get resources to help. When I receive a large amount of food or anything I share with my neighbors because we need to help each other if we can. We pray together to win this battle to show our children how keeping God first in our life can make everything possible. Our purpose is not just about hearing an awesome message and keeping quiet. We must learn to share with others who are not believers and let them know that God wants us to be good disciples for him.

God please help me walk in victory and teach me to wait until I hear your voice. I need you to help me through when I don't see anything happening because my flesh is starting to get weak. God please talk me through, so I won't make a dumb or stupid move. Thank you, God, for hiding me when the devil tried to kill me. Some people want to see me fail, but I have God. He is in control and I am not in this by myself. Nothing is stronger than a deep praying mother and an awesome pastor praying for you and your family. You have to stay linked to greatness and a few real people praying with you because prayer changes things. I try to apply every message I hear to my life. It is an everyday battle, but I stay prayed up. I'm not going to give up. I'm going to wait on God's voice to make my next move.

Thank you, God, for watching over me and your love for me. This has helped me get through life knowing I am walking in faith, even if I am not seeing where I'm going. I'm holding on to your unchanging hand. Thank you, God, for never giving up on me. Thank you for never leaving me. Thank you for saving my children, giving me peace to sleep, and to know you are covering them because you are in control of all things. Thank you, God, for helping me to let go and stop trying to rescue my children. I just get weak sometimes allowing my emotions to lead me in the wrong direction. Knowing you see all my pain helps me endure on a daily basis.

Thank you, God, for teaching me to love people always, even those who want to say mean things because they are bored. People have hurt me with gossip about other church members. Some act like they are better than other people. The God I serve loves everyone, no matter what or how they look. Come the way you are to His kingdom. It is our place of healing, a place to get some encouragement and knowledge of His word so we can bless someone else. I am so thankful that God loves me.

I enjoy teaching the children when I come in the morning. They always say good morning I love you teacher. They even look for me when I'm not there. That's real love. I enjoy helping them with life skills like, how to write their names, to paint, to cut paper, build things with wooden blocks, to share with each other and be kind. God gave me this gift to be a blessing and I love it. So many have grown up and gone off to college. I am so thankful that I had a hand in that. When I see the parents, they always say thank you to me for being in their child's life. It hasn't been easy, but I press my way through everyday because they are always watching to see me come through that door. They are my biggest fans. I like to push them when they are being lazy. We sing songs together while we have circle time and they like to stand up to sing out loud for the group. I am so proud of them. We share our supplies with the class next door and help the new teachers that come in to be a part of our family. We also have foster grandparents that come to help out. They enjoy working with the children and they help us a lot. Thank you, God, for putting all these great children in my life. It's awesome to be trusted.

The Next Chapter

I want to talk about what I've been through in the last year. I had to have surgery and that was a very hard choice because I have never been cut like this. I had to keep going back to the doctors to get different tests to make sure I didn't have any cancer on the thyroid on both sides of my neck. After the last appointment I decided to have my thyroid removed because I had three more growths on the left side. Now I have to take a pill for the rest of my life, but I'm adjusting to it. Sometimes it's hard because we don't see a change right away. I know God promised to be with me all the days of my life. All things work together for the good of his people. I am on my way to greatness. This is my season. I have been through so much and know it's my time. He took his time making me so good to bring out the best in me. When you are praying for something and it looks like it's not going to happen, the devil will try to block it. Don't be afraid because God will bless you. So, don't change and don't stop being nice to people and helping them because God will reward you for your good work. Just be cautious of the people you let in on this journey. Not everyone has your best interest. Stay prayed up at all times because you will be attacked. My weapon is my prayer.

Sometimes I thank God for helping me make it from point A to B. It's hard fighting the battle day to day. I have become more careful about the people I let into my life, so I tend to avoid people that have a lot of wicked things going on. When I let them in, I become connected to all that madness. I didn't look at it that way until I went through it. Thank you, God, for showing up to save me. If it doesn't feel right, you better not go there. That's your inner spirit speaking to you. Sometimes it is better to tell yourself no. Nowadays it's hard to trust anyone. You better think about it before you leap into the deep end. It's easy to get in, but hard to get out. That's real. At times you'll find yourself questioning what you got yourself into and praying to God to help you find your way out of the mess. You promise not to act on the desires of the flesh again. I get weak sometimes. I'm so happy I don't act on my bad thoughts. I ask God to help me because I can't do it alone. I know I'm not in this by myself.

People call me and tell me all kinds of lies. It's just a mess. I don't want to hear it. Sometimes I don't even answer my phone. I changed my number. I had to. I'm on a different level now. I can't operate the same way or think the same or be around the same people either. When you go through a transformation, you just don't go to the places you used to or do the things you used to. You don't allow the same mess in again. It was a lesson learned. I don't want to repeat any heartache. God taught me how to forgive and not be bitter. I'm moving forward with my vision to serve others. I stay close to the Lord's voice and not my own flesh. I look deeper when people say they want to be connected to me. I don't want any more people around me that are not willing to chase after your word and pray with me. We will be stronger in our walk only by praying and staying true to your word daily and by being a blessing to others. People have been calling me a fool for sharing my life.

Some people are funny. They won't treat you right when they are in a relationship with you. All it takes is for you to move on with your life for them to realize what they had. Sometimes you have to lose what you have to appreciate that person for their quality. I thank God I am stronger today to deal with people lying to me about silly things because it's not worth it and there's no need to even react to it. I just keep praying for God to help me through everything in my life. I can't make it without Him in my life. He has been so awesome to me and my family. This is what helps me to stay focused every day. I'm envisioning more great things as I serve others. I'm praying for God to send only those players that will follow the lead. We won't always agree, but we have to be going in the same direction to make things happen together. We need to be bold because we will see different things coming from all directions, but if we keep praying together, we will be alright through God's grace.

As I look back at some of the childish behavior that I allowed from a man, I am so glad God closed those doors. Some people from my past are still the same or worse. People question why I go to church so much. I love it. My faith keeps me strong. They invite me to hang out. I say we can at my church and suddenly, the conversation changes. I recall how one man who was interested in me started coming to church. I started talking to God about it. I asked if this is the one because he was doing everything right . I soon found out he was attending the service just to get what he wanted. I was supposed to stop seeing him, but I didn't. It was my mistake to keep allowing him to take up anymore of my time. I was thinking with my flesh. I wasn't prayed up and I acted on emotions. I try really hard to stay prayed up and focused on this journey. I'm happy it's my past and not my present. I thank God for keeping me in a place of peace with my life. I am more mature today. Because His grace and mercy covers me, I stepped out to help my loved ones because it was the right thing to do, and because I love them. I am learning that sometimes even your loved ones will hurt you. I'm going to hand them over to God. He can handle it better than me. I don't need any more drama. I'll just keep praying for them. Some people you just can't help. You have to change your life and have a different mindset to be a blessing to others. If the people around you are holding you from what you need to do, then you need to let them go. Ask God to increase your faith and remove the bitterness. You may have to forgive them. People will try to break you down because you are doing something that they are afraid to do.

I keep going to church because that's my hospital. You have to be in a good church. When you hear a preacher, you should feel something. If you are not receiving what you need or feel better than you did when you got there, either you weren't listening or it's not the right place for you. Sometimes the choir can bless you with a song if the they can sing. I enjoy the singing. I do my holy dance. Sometimes I find it hard to be still when the spirit touches me. It's like fire in my bones. Sometimes when I'm riding in my car, listening to gospel music, I start crying because just hearing the name Jesus blesses me so much. When I used to sing in the church choir, I loved it a lot. We would have nice programs and visit other churches. I traveled to nice places like Los Angeles. It was my first time going there. It was a nice city. It was a very big church with a lot of people. I was nervous. We had never gone to a church as big as that, but it was a blessing to experience that with my church. I wish I had the vision I have now back then because we were right next to Hollywood, but God knew it wasn't my time.

I learned something new again. What I'm looking at is not what's going to be for me. It's just a choice I must make. People from my past are starting to call me, talking about wanting to spend time with me. I find it difficult to understand because it's been many years. I ask myself why they are calling after all I have endured. I have survived all the pain without you. Now here you come. If it wasn't so tragic, it would be funny. Well, it's not happening. I'm staying focused on my blessings. People always want to come back after all the struggles are over. They just want to enjoy the fun part of your journey. When you needed someone to help you, no one was there to offer any help. To those people I say, "you should have been trying to talk to me a long time ago. I still show love because that's what I have to do so I don't mess up the blessings God has waiting for me. I thank God for my maturity because if I didn't have this growth, I would have choked a lot of people. I let God fight my battle for me.

I want my children to see and understand that only prayers will bring you out of all the bad choices you make in life. I say, "believe in Him and the word with all your heart and wait on God." Because we like to see things change right away, we must remember God moves in His own time. Sometimes He won't change the problem. He will just change us to see if we learn from the last bad choice. Sometimes we end up repeating the same thing until we realize that our way is not working. I am learning not to worry about everything. Thank you, God, for all my blessings. I just want to be a blessing and to serve others.

I am reminded of how hard it was living in the housing project. I remember how the walls had mildew everywhere. I wrote a letter to the board leaders to help me and we went to city hall to meet with some powerful people in office to help my kids and I move out to a better place. It took me four to five years of going back and forth to city hall. People were getting killed around us. Robbery and drug dealers coming around looking for people that owed them money were a regular thing. They would shoot up the place like there weren't families living there.

I finally received a letter saying my family would be granted section 8 so we could find a better place to live. We were given money to move. You can't tell me God is not real. If he blessed me and my kids this way, He can do the same for you. So never give up because everything we need God knows it. God will always give you a plan to make it out.

Don't look at people and what they are doing. You can't change anything or anybody. You can only control and change yourself. Have you ever felt like getting away from certain people because they get on your nerves? Have you ever wished you could move because the place you live is full of people who don't appreciate you? Have you ever been in love with someone who is always complaining and just being mean? Have you ever had children that didn't listen and ended up in jail and hurting your heart? Have you ever had experiences that make you so angry? Have you ever felt like you just need to get out because you have been trapped for a long time and need to be blessed to get out? Have you ever felt like you just don't have any way out? I have.

God always has an abundance of deliverance. God will raise you for greatness. Some of the people that used to be your friend won't understand where He is taking your life. I want to be a blessing to my kids because I love them so much. It's not easy, but you can do it. God made you this way to be able to handle it.

Maybe its means you need to leave some people behind. Some people are only there for a season. I am trying my best to do what's right so God will see the glory of my service to others. I think if I had given up on moving forward with my book, I would have been sending a message to my followers that giving up is what you should do. I don't want to let myself down or the single moms who look up to me. I have to watch everything I do and say because they are watching. We encourage each other. When they need me to just listen, I do. When they need housing resources or a ride somewhere, I try my best to provide it. Sometimes it's enough to let them know that I've been through that, and God saved me. He will do the same for them. He's faithful. He will never let you down. Don't worry about what people might say. I will be praying day and night for your life to be great. Don't be afraid. There will be some stumbling blocks in your path. Just look up to the heavens where all our help comes from and remember that only what we do for God will count. I am on my way to writing many more books and being a blessing to people all over the world. This has been a new challenge in my life. Now I know I can do anything through God's grace and love and faith. He is so awesome in my life. There are so many people to thank for supporting me.

The Journey Forward

When I first decided to start writing I had no idea how hard it was going to be, but through prayer and God's grace I started. Sometimes I cry when I think back on all the hard and painful situations I've had to endure. I was not alone through all these, God was there with me, saving my mind and saving my life.

I never thought I could share my precious moments and experiences with an audience. I pray it blesses many. Just think about God's grace in my life. I've really come a long way from not knowing how I'm going to put food on the table, or how to get money to buy new shoes, how to buy a jacket because it's winter , how to pay the rent after being in the hospital and having all my money tied up in the computers because someone didn't do their job right, to where I am today. We can do all things through God's strength.

God has a plan for my life that is bigger than me. I can't do anything without him. The closer I get to my purpose; the more things start going off track in a bid to distract me. I know I am on the crux of my blessings. So, I'll keep moving forward. I know others won't be happy for me and some won't understand what I'm going through, but it's ok. I have to stay focused on my purpose.

Sometimes things happen that I can't explain. I have to connect myself with people that want to see greatness in me not just take the fruit of my labor. Not everyone knows the struggles I went through or the circumstances I had to face on my journey, but I made it through God's mercy at my darkest time. I thought I was not going to make it, but he saw greatness in me even when I didn't. I'm learning to do what I can and letting go of what I can't control. It's hard because the conflicts keep coming my way. I pray to make better choices. I'm learning to be careful of who I let into my space. I know I am not in this by myself. I thank God I am not where I used to be. My children don't understand what God is doing in my life. I don't either, but sometimes I just trust in him with all my heart and faith. I am still standing. I have evidence of my journey. I know that God has brought me from a mighty long way.

I want more now. Before now, I used to settle, but not anymore. I know I am the prize. So, if you want me, you have to be willing to grow with me. You can't be selfish. Loving people is hard work. I have to do things differently in this season so I can attain my destiny. There are times when I wonder why things had to be so hard and rough. It definitely made me stronger and brought me closer to God.

The Breakdown

One day I started screaming very loud and my children woke up. I scared them. They started crying. I told them it's going to be okay; just get me to the hospital. In the car, it felt like my body was being lifting up. I asked God to help me. I didn't understand why this was happening. My children were calling all the family to come to the hospital to be with us. I was so crazy. I couldn't feel my body. It was like I was floating, and my eyes were rolling over. The nurse asked what happened. I tried to explain it to her, but it wasn't coming out right. The nurse gave me a shot to calm me down. My children were still crying. I wanted to tell them that mom is going to be ok.

The next thing I knew I was lying in bed in a hospital room. I laid down, looking around. I asked God what was going on. My heart was pumping so fast. They put me on a heart machine to monitor my heart rate. I was a mess. The doctor came in to talk with me. He said I had a big thyroid goiter on my neck. I asked what that was. I asked if this is why my heart was pumping so fast. I thought I was about to die. He chuckled and said I wasn't going to die. He told me I had an anxiety attack. I asked where that came from. It was scary. He said stress is the biggest factor, but sometimes it can be from drinking or using different drugs. I told him I don't drink, and I don't use drugs. I didn't know what was happening to me. It was crazy. One minute I was asleep and the next, some overwhelming feeling woke me up from my sleep. The medicine they administered to calm me down is the same stuff they give to people suffering from depression. My body wasn't used to that. It was a life changing experience. I couldn't work. I didn't want to eat. I just laid down because my body was so weak. I couldn't smell anything and when I did, it made me sick to my stomach. I was having crazy thoughts.

I kept praying to God, asking him to please keep me alive. I wanted to be with my family. I had gotten so small because I couldn't eat. The medicine was making me nauseous. I couldn't hold anything in. I didn't understand why all this was happening to me. I could hear a loud voice talking to me and saying God is with you. So, don't worry. He loves you so much. Keep fighting for your life.

I was having crazy thoughts about dying. The medication was so strong considering the fact that it was such a little tablet. I prayed to God to help me get off this stuff. It was too powerful for my body. I stopped taking it and I started experiencing that weird feeling again. I went running back to the doctor because I wasn't used to that. I wanted to be able to smell and eat again. I didn't feel the same. They gave me new medication. It was like been born again. I had to learn how to keep food in my stomach. I just wanted to get back to a normal life, but my healing took time. The doctors wanted to lock me up because of the way that medicine had me reacting to. I told God if he got me off this medicine, I'll stop stressing about things I don't have control over. I wanted my life back. He blessed me and took me off that bad medication. I thank God for healing me from that experience. It showed me that even at my darkest hour, He was right there with me. As the days went by, I started feeling better. I was beginning to perceive again and was able to eat food without getting an upset stomach. God has been so awesome in my life. I tell people I don't look like what I've been through.

I'm so thankful that my children love me and for their prayers. Thank you for taking care of your mom. I didn't know how to be mom. I had to learn to be one by trial and error. I am thankful to God for always being in my life. I'm thankful that He always shows up when nobody else does.

I hope my book blesses everyone that reads it. If you want to do something, be bold and do it. Believe in yourself. I have been wanting to write this book since my mom died. I thank God for inspiring me. Only by His grace am I able to do this. He taught me to listen more and love no matter how people treat me. My purpose on this earth is to serve others with love. When things are done out of love, it works for the good of everyone connected. Working with teenagers is my passion. I worked at the group home for two years.

We became very close. Some of them didn't have any contact with their family for different reasons. I would show love to them and listen to them. I encouraged them to pray about everything they go through. I shared my journey with them. I let them know that there will always be people who will doubt them simply because they are afraid to step out on faith. Don't look at them. Keep your mind on God.

People will look at you crazy and say mean things about you behind your back. They will tell others not to talk to you. They will question why you are trying to help others and start your own company. They wonder how you can do that when you don't have a good education, or a husband. They will even go as far as saying your children are off the hook. One thing I can say is that I do have a father who owns everything, and he told me if I seek Him first, He will add great things to my life. I just have to stay humble on my journey. People will bring up your past to try to distract you, but I tell them that's ok. I'm still standing.

Grief is a painful and powerful process. Losing people you love back to back is rough. Not knowing where you are going to sleep or how you are going to get around because you lost your car and your bank account is overwhelming. When the people around you don't offer you any kind of love or help, it's crushing. God didn't turn his back on me. I stayed faithful.

I got a new car. I got a new place to live. I got a new job and those people that mocked me were still looking, but they weren't laughing anymore. They started asking how I was getting all these things so fast. I told them God gave it to me. They don't want to believe it. This is my reward for praying and trusting in His word. God never fails me. Trouble doesn't always last. You will see the light again. Always follow your first instinct. If your mind says don't go right, don't do it. That's the spirit inside you keeping you safe.

My children act like they don't have any common sense. I have done the best I know how to love them, cook, clean, teach them about God's greatness in mine and in their life. It is only through God's grace and mercy that we made it. Sometimes I just don't know where I went wrong as a mother. I see things in my children that hurt me deeply. I pray daily for them.

I went back to work. I am glad about that because I was missing my kids. They are my life. When I walk inside my classroom, they greet me so wonderfully. They run and give me hugs, and say "I love you teacher." That helps me heal faster. Having them in my life is like having a second family. My coworkers calling me to ask me how I am doing was so uplifting. Having them offer their support and bring me supplies when it was needed was so nice.

Things got crazy with my money. The hospital gave me the wrong forms and it took so long to get things right. No one told me that I had do my own footwork while I was trying to heal. I started crying and praying, and then things got better. I didn't get money until the next year after I had my surgery. Thank you, God, for saving me through the madness!

What I've Been Through

I want to share the story of how I survived domestic violence. In the beginning things were great. We were holding hands, going out on the town, meeting family and friends, playing card games, having dinners with everyone, and going to church together. We were enjoying life. My friends were very supportive of me, but they didn't really care for him because he was very controlling. I didn't see it that way. My daddy was gone already. My dad always told me that no man has the right to control me or hit me, but I didn't pay attention. After a while, things started getting crazy.

The lying, not coming home when he was supposed to, the red marks on his neck were all red flags. When I questioned this, he turned it on me and got mad, and started a fight with me. I looked at him like he was crazy. He was coming home with red marks on him and lying to me about where he was. I'd start crying and asking myself why he was doing those things. I was cleaning and cooking, taking care of the children and doing things I don't like to please him. This was my reward for that. I started to question my sanity.

I would talk with my girlfriend about it and she told me to leave him. I told her I couldn't. We have a family. Maybe he won't do it again because he says he loves me and his kids. He even made a big show of ending it in front of me. He called her in front of me. He told her he couldn't see her anymore because he loved his family. I thought, wow, he really cares for us. At that time, I didn't have the courage to do what I needed to. About two months later, I came out my door and to my surprise I see this same girl. I was heated. She was friends with our neighbors.

It was all so awful. I even talked to the girl to find out how she knew him and to tell her he wasn't any good. People told me to stay with him. They said that's how men are. If he's providing for you and your kids, don't leave him. That's such bad advice. I knew then it was time for me to make better choices. I called the police and they told him to leave. He left and was gone for about two months.

He asked to come back home and like a fool I let him. I should never have done that, but I wasn't making good choices at that point. He started acting even more crazy than before. I didn't know this man. I knew if one of us didn't leave, someone was going to lose their life. He was on some new level of abuse. I don't know what kind of people he was hanging out with, but it was not good for anyone. He was just so different. He was always going out. I don't know what that was about. He would come back so angry and refuse to talk about it. He just kept hitting the wall and yelling "fuck". He hid things from me. That's what caused a lot of our relationship problems. I told him he needed to leave. He said he wasn't going anywhere. He said I should leave. I wasn't going anywhere without my children. I told him I didn't trust him because he was so angry, and I was scared he might do something he would be sorry for later.

I went upstairs to get my purse. He came behind me and tried getting close to me, but I didn't want to be close to him. He got mad. I don't know what went wrong, but we were fighting so fast. He was choking my neck and my son came running upstairs yelling to leave his mom alone. He just turned around and looked at him. He kept yelling and hitting the wall saying I just didn't know. At that time, I didn't want to know anything. I just wanted him out because it was not a good situation for us. The police came again to make him leave. He didn't want to go. The police didn't care which one of us left, but someone had to. My son was so hurt, seeing his mom get hurt in a terrible way at such a young age. He didn't deserve that.

When I tell people about the things that happened, they look at me and say, "damn, you don't look like you been abused and beaten." They wondered how I went through that and didn't have any black eyes, scrapes or cuts on my face. I told them it was God's grace and I fought back for my life. I learned not to love anyone more than myself. All abuse hurts. I prayed a lot and that helped me not to give up the battle for my life. If you are reading this and going through anything similar, I want you to know that God will never let you down no matter how the fight is set up. He will save you. You must love yourself enough to fight back. Fighting doesn't necessarily mean physical, but more of a spiritual fight. We have to understand that we must think right to make things better in our lives. My life has been one of constant struggle, but through God's grace I am still standing for greatness.

It took me time to heal from my mom's death. I had to get mentally prepared to write and move forward with my goal. People ask how I was able to deal with all the hardships. The answer is prayer and never giving up. I went to church and asked my pastor to pray for me. I went to bible study. I stayed connected to my church family. I have great people praying for me and an awesome prayer partner.

When I told my children about writing this book they didn't know how to respond. I hope that watching me write and type this work will give them hope that dreams can come true. If you make up your mind to make it happen, it will. I tell my children to learn as much as they can because in this world you need to learn everything that you can to be all you need to be. I want so much for my children. That is why I'm working so hard on my book to be even more of a blessing to them. I want them to always have hope and dream big. We don't realize how much God prepares us to handle what comes our way. It is not to hurt us, but for us to learn from it. I pray to God for a changed mind. I'm glad that I know to value myself first and not to settle for less. I can do fine by myself. I have peace of mind.

I'm getting ready for my greatness. I'm so excited to share and be a blessing so God will be glorified. The windows of heaven will open for me and my kids for my faithfulness. When I go out of my way to help others, I am so happy because God always puts people in my life to help me. My kids are always asking me why I take food and give it to others when we don't even have enough for ourselves. I tell them that the people I'm helping don't have anything. God wants us to help others. I believe we have to think about others before ourselves because there is always someone worse off. I listen to people when they talk and hear their need. I bless them in some kind of way and my joy comes from seeing the smile on their faces. I want to help so many others. There is so much suffering around the world. Don't say what you can't do. Focus on what you can do.

Don't react to any negativity that comes your way. Whatever you need God has already done it. That's why when you go to apply for a job or for an apartment, the only thing you do is walk in and start talking as you fill out the paperwork. The next thing you know, the person tells you he or she is going to give you a chance because you have great potential. That is God's favor every time. Thank you for always hooking your daughter up! You must go to church to get fed. I can't live without it. I am learning not to react when haters bring up my past. I just bless them and move on.

I have a big vision and I'm doing it with no help and no money. God said I need to bring it myself. It's like an ant pulling something big. That's what I'm doing. I'm pulling something bigger than me. I have to keep going. My reward is coming soon. Great things come in small packages. I can be happy with that and be a blessing to someone else. God will bless you more for your willing and humble heart. I must reposition myself, so I don't repeat the same habits. I closed the book on my past. I am busy with awesome things. I believe that dreams come true. God said I shall have it. I have been through enough heartache in my life. God is getting to show me things my eyes have never seen or my mind has only imagined. I know I'm very close.

I stay on my knees praying because prayer changes things. This time when the wind blows my way, I'm not going to let my opportunity pass me by. I'm so excited about my journey. I love to love because God is love. I've been loving people I don't even know. They say I'm always smiling and that I'm such a bubbly person. I tell them it's all God. He's been so good to me and my children.

As women, we need to help each other more, listen and support each other, and be a good friend. We must learn to forgive and let go. I'm really doing things out of the box. The windows of heaven are opening for me and my kids. I must keep doing what's right. It may take a while before you see a change, but it will come when you're not thinking about it.

If you want anything in life, you have to be ready for hard work. Some people will start treating you different. Don't worry about them. You deserve what you are being blessed with. You must be very bold in every area to make it happen. Favor ain't fair sometimes. I need to be around good people. I've already had my share of crazy ones. Be willing to leave poisonous people alone so you can move forward. I have been hurt so bad by mean people. I wanted to kill them. Yes, that's a lot of anger. That's real. I'm a human being with feelings. Stay prayed up. I'm good and I hope you will be too. God bless you all. Thank you for supporting me and loving me.

It took time, but it happened. I'm so blessed and so grateful for my family. Family is first, even when they don't work, don't clean up, won't stop the kids for running around breaking up things, eating up the food, going to jail, getting drunk and wanting to fight with everyone. I don't understand it all, but I still love them. We pray together no matter what. My siblings and I started having brother and sister lunches so we can stay connected to each other. We talk about our kids, what they are doing, how they are staying out of trouble and if they are working. We are planning more events so we can stay closer. My auntie taught me to always be nice and stay close to God. All I have is because God blesses me.

I remember needing a new car and not having the money or even good credit. I went to this place I saw on TV. They said they help everybody. I was there for hours, not getting any help. They ran my credit over and over again. I wanted to leave. A tall, handsome man came over to me and asked me how I was doing. I told him I was fine, but getting ready to leave because all I had been doing was waiting around. He said he would find out what was going on. I started praying and he asked me what I was doing. I told him. Then he said he was going to say a prayer for me too. About an hour later he told me to come to his office. He had good news. He told me I would be going home in my new car. I started shouting in his office. I thanked God for my blessing because it was completely due to His grace. Nothing is too hard for God. I am a living testimony. I know I'm on the right path. God will reward you for your good works.

Staying Faithful

I'm going to share some more stories about how awesome God has been in my life. I have been talking with so many famous people without even realizing. One day I'm just being me and talking with people and the next I look up on tv and there they are. God is really putting great people in my path.

I enjoy going out in the early morning to pass out clothes to the homeless. I am not afraid because I know God is with me. The people are so thankful to see my friend and I coming. They call us the church ladies. They ask us to pray for them and if we can come back to bring more clothes and food to them. This is what God wants us to do. I hope I'm showing my children to always help others and to do it with a smile. God will reward them for it.

I'm so excited to help my single moms. We are like family. They come looking for me when they don't see me to share with me what's going on in their lives. Sometimes I just listen and pray with them. This is what I live for. Sharing about my journey with other women. I'm moving forward with my purpose to be a blessing to someone else. To God be the glory. I think about the losses in my life and I realize they've all made me stronger. I know now that God had that in His plan and had an angel lined up to take over so my siblings and I will be alright.

God loved me and never gave up on me even when people thought I was crazy. He knew that I would heal with his mercy and divine grace when the time is right. Thank you, God. Everything in the name of Jesus. Now I'm just praying for honest people in my path because I've had my share of fake people in my life. I want to be more than just a church goer. I want to be linked to quality people who pray faithfully, so that when I'm in need of something or need someone to pray with me, we can share the blessing of God together and lift each other while staying connected to God.

God didn't save me for me to just sit down. I have to share with the world the greatness he has done in my life. I'm hoping it will bless someone out there. I didn't know I would be sharing my life with the world, but God did. I'm not ashamed about anything God has saved me from. I'm learning to let problems go and let God take control.

At the group home, we would have dinner together. We also had check-in time to see how the day went. If there was anybody who wanted to share something with the group, they did. Some girls liked to talk away from the group. The girls had a schedule to follow. There were always some people who didn't respect that. We would do bed checks and if they went AWOL, we had to call the police to report them missing. They always found them close by. They weren't really trying to run away. They just wanted attention.

I had to watch over them and the babies. We sometimes got calls from the hospital to come pick up newborn babies because crack was found in the mother's blood. I loved taking care of the babies. The girls and I would make food together. There was a nice big kitchen for it. We enjoyed allowing the girls to share the few good memories they had. We always tried to stay positive. I kept loving on them. To this day I still see some of the children I have supported, and I can see the love they have for me when they look at me and smile. And when they reach out to give me a hug and introduce me to their families, I know then that I have been a blessing. I like it when different parents come up to me and say I look the same when I'm shopping at the mall with my kids. They tell me it's because of me that their son is in college. That's when I feel so blessed that I was a part of such greatness.

I just love the young people. I'm so blessed that God trusts me with all the lives I have blessed and made a difference in. I will help wherever I can and whoever I can. If I don't have what they need, I will help find it. This is what we are here for, to help our people and serve each other. As Black, single women, we need to build each other up and help out in every area. We need to let our children see us working together and getting along like the great women we say we are. When others see us trying to be better, it will give them hope to do the same. It's all part of God's plan for all to be as one.

It's a fixed fight and I have already won the fight. I'm on the winning team, and that's God's team. Even if I might have some struggles, I will still make it. I know some people turned their backs on me, but it's ok because God will cover me through all my battles. This is why I ask God for help through everything. I do all things in love, even for people I don't know. That's stepping out of the box when you can show love to people that have hurt you. I pray for God to bless me because I love doing what's right. I might fall short sometimes, but I will get back up and do better next time. Quitting is not in my life or plan.

Thank you for reading my story. I hope it blesses you in a great way. Don't worry. God is with you. Just love on people. The hardest thing to do is stay prayed up. Please keep me in your prayers that God will continue to bless me to keep reaching out and being a blessing to others.

Stay tuned...my next book is coming soon.

God bless you!

About the Author

Charlotte Pinkney is a single mother of three kids from Palakta, Florida. She always puts God first. You can reach out to her via Instagram @charlotte_stay_blessed or by email at mspinkneyblessed@gmail.com.